MARTIN LUTHER

Martin Luther

The Reformer

John Ritchie

JOHN RITCHIE LTD
CHRISTIAN PUBLICATIONS

40 Beansburn, Kilmarnock, Scotland

ISBN-13: 978 1 909803 88 6

Copyright © 2014 by John Ritchie Ltd.
40 Beansburn, Kilmarnock, Scotland

www.ritchiechristianmedia.co.uk

All rights reserved. No part of this publication may be reproduced, stored in a retrievable system, or transmitted in any form or by any other means – electronic, mechanical, photocopy, recording or otherwise – without prior permission of the copyright owner.

Typeset by John Ritchie Ltd., Kilmarnock
Printed by Bell & Bain Ltd., Glasgow

CONTENTS

CHAPTER		PAGE
1.	Early Days	9
2.	The Student at Erfurt	17
3.	The Monk	23
4.	Luther at Wittenberg	31
5.	The Visit to Rome	37
6.	The Indulgences	45
7.	The Theses	53
8.	Augsburg	63
9.	A Truce	73
10.	The Papal Bull	81
11.	The Diet of Worms	89
12.	The Wartburg	103
13.	Return to Wittenberg	111
14.	Closing Scenes	121

EARLY DAYS

Chapter 1

EARLY DAYS

My Father, Thou art the guide of my youth.—
Jer. 3:4.

MARTIN LUTHER was born on November 10, 1483, in the little town of Eisleben, in Saxony. His parents were very poor; they feared God, and lived uprightly. John Luther, his father, was a woodcutter. Often his mother, Margaret, carried wood upon her back, so that she might help to get the means for bringing up her children.

When the little boy was about six months old, his parents left Eisleben, and went to live at Mansfeld. Here for some time John Luther worked as a miner, and by steady perseverance managed to save sufficient money to purchase two small furnaces for smelting iron. He was a man fond of books, and sought the society of learned men. Soon afterward, he was made a member of the town council of Mansfeld, and was able to invite to his table the learned men of the place. The clergy and the schoolmasters were frequent guests. While these dined with his father, young Martin was allowed to remain in the room.

This greatly pleased him, for it was his ambition to become a schoolmaster or a learned man.

As soon as their son was old enough to be taught, his parents sought to teach him to know God, and to train the child up in His fear. Often his father would kneel by his bedside and pray aloud, asking the Lord that his boy might remember His name, and one day contribute to the propagation of the truth.

We shall see how the good father's prayers were answered.

While still very young, the lad was sent to school, and often little Martin was carried in his father's arms, or in the arms of a friend, to the schoolmaster's house. We do not know whether he liked school; perhaps he did not, for the discipline was very severe. He was clever, but impetuous and sometimes obstinate. Often, both at home and at school, he was severely chastised. His mother on one occasion beat him severely and his schoolmaster flogged him fifteen times one morning. Relating this latter incident, many years afterward, he said, "We must whip children, but we must also love them."

At school he was taught the catechism, the Ten Commandments, the Apostle's Creed, the Lord's Prayer, and a little Latin; but his thoughts were not directed to God, and his only religious sentiment at this time was fear. When the gentle Saviour was spoken of, he turned pale with fright; for as yet he knew Him only as an angry Judge.

John Luther wished to make his son a scholar, so, when he was fourteen years old, he was taken from

Early Days

the school at Mansfeld, and sent to a better one at Magdeburg, a town not very far away. His mother was sorry to part with him, but she gave her consent, and he left home to enter upon his new studies. A young friend went with him, whose name was John Reinke.

The two boys were not happy at this school. A lad of fourteen, thrown upon the world without friends or protectors, Luther trembled when in the presence of his masters, and when his studies were over he painfully begged his bread in company with children poorer than himself. One day, about Christmas time, they were wandering through the neighboring villages singing pretty carols of the infant Jesus. Cold and hungry, they stopped before a peasant's cottage, hoping that some kind person hearing them sing would come and give them food to eat. "Where are you boys?" cried out a harsh voice. The boys were frightened, and ran away as fast as their legs would carry them. The farmer followed; he had a harsh voice but a kind heart, and, calling them back, he gave them food, for which they were very grateful.

After being at Magdeburg about a year, his parents sent him to a preparatory school at Eisenach. This they did because they had heard of the difficulty which he found in supporting himself, and as his father had relatives living in the town to which he was going, John Luther hoped they would help to support Martin. They, however, took no responsibility for him. When pinched by hunger he had to sing and beg at Eisenach, as he had done before at Magdeburg.

Martin loved his studies, and God, who so kindly watches over us, did not forget the friendless boy. One day, having been turned away from three houses, he was standing still, feeling very sad, before the door of a worthy citizen. Must he leave his studies, and return to labor with his father in the mines of Mansfeld? Suddenly a door opened, and a woman appeared. It was Ursula, the wife of Conrad Cotta, the burgomaster of the city. She had often heard the lad's sweet voice, and remarked his attentive behavior in church. Seeing him standing so sad before her door, she spoke kindly to him, brought him into the house, and set food before him. Conrad, when he came home, entirely approved of what his good wife had done, and found so much pleasure in the boy's society that he took him to live in his house.

Here he lived very peacefully for about five years. He was so cheerful and obliging that all who knew him loved him. He learned to play the flute and the lute. Accompanying his fine alto voice by the lute, he took special delight in testifying by his melody his gratitude to his adopted mother, who was very fond of music. His love for his kind protectors was great, and it is pleasing to read that many years afterward, when Martin Luther was the great and learned doctor of Wittenberg, he joyfully received one of their sons, who came to that city to study, into his house.

Remembering the kind Ursula, he said: "There is nothing sweeter on earth than the heart of a woman in which piety dwells." His own heart was strengthened, and his confidence in God so deeply rooted that the severest trials could not afterward shake it.

While under Conrad's roof, the strength of his understanding, the liveliness of his imagination, and the excellence of his memory, carried him beyond all his schoolmates. He made rapid progress, especially in Latin, in eloquence, and in poetry.

> God is our refuge in distress,
> Our shield of hope through every care,
> Our Shepherd watching us to bless,
> And therefore will we not despair;
> Although the mountains shake,
> And hills their place forsake,
> And billows o'er them break,
> Yet still will we not fear,
> For Thou, O God, art ever near.
> M. L.

THE STUDENT AT ERFURT

Chapter 2

THE STUDENT AT ERFURT

The fear of the Lord is the beginning of knowledge.—Prov. 1:7.

Luther was now eighteen, a young man earnestly thirsting for knowledge. His father wished him to study law, and hoped great things for his talented son. He sent him to the University of Erfurt. This was in 1501. Here he attentively studied the philosophy of the Middle Ages, and read Cicero, Virgil, and other classic authors. The whole university admired his genius; but even at this time he did not learn merely to cultivate the intellect and win worldly fame. A deeper importance began to attach itself to his studies, and those serious thoughts and that heart directed heavenward, which God gives to those whom He purposes to make His most zealous ministers, were his. He felt his dependence upon God, and earnestly asked His blessing upon all that he engaged in. "To pray well," he said, "is the better half of study."

All his spare time he spent in the library of the university—and a new impulse and direction were about to be given his desires. One day, when he had been at Erfurt about two years, he was taking down book after book, looking at the authors' names. One in particular attracted his attention. Holding it in his hands, he read the title—paused—read again. A Bible! a rare book, unknown in those days. He opened its pages, and the story of Hannah and young Samuel was before him. His soul was full of joy as he read it, and he returned home with the thought: "Oh, if God would give me such a book for my own!" Day after day found him in the library reading the newly discovered treasure.

At this time he twice narrowly escaped death. His severe study brought on a dangerous illness, and his friends thought that he would die. He feared so himself. To a kind old priest who visited him, he said, "Soon I shall be called away from this world." But the old man replied, "My dear bachelor, take courage; you will not die of this illness. Our God will yet make of you a man who, in turn, shall console many."

Shortly after, he was going home to spend a short time with his parents, and, according to the custom of the age, wore a sword. The blade accidentally fell out, and cut one of his principal arteries. The blood gushed forth. His companion fled for assistance, and Luther, left alone, lay down on his back, trying in vain to stop the bleeding by pressing his finger upon the wound. Thinking death was near he cried, "O Mary, help me!" He then trusted in Mary; later on, his only trust was in Jesus.

Yet another event occurred to direct his thoughts to the subject of death. A dear friend, named Alexis,

The Student at Erfurt

was assassinated. He was very much grieved, and said, "What would become of me if I were thus called away without warning?"

While his father was urging him to study law, his heart told him that religion was the one thing needful, and his thoughts turned toward a monastic life. He felt that if he were shut out from the world he would become holy, and that the sins which troubled him so much would depart.

It is 1505, and Luther has been made Master of Arts and Doctor of Philosophy. We see that he is becoming a learned man.

He has again paid his parents a visit, and is returning to Erfurt. When a short distance from that city a violent thunder-storm comes on. The lightning flashes, the thunder roars, the bolt seems to fall at his feet. He is greatly terrified, and falls upon his knees. Death, the judgment, eternity, are all present before him. He makes a solemn vow that if God will spare him, he will forsake the world and devote himself to religion. The storm passes away, and he rises from his knees. The sun shines, but darkness remains upon his heart. He feels that he must become holy; but how? As yet he knows nothing of the cleansing power of Jesus' blood. To become a monk is his idea of finding holiness.

He enters Erfurt again, and one evening he invites his college friends to a cheerful but frugal supper. All are happy; but while the merry talk goes on, Luther tells them of his resolve. They are sad, and beg him not to go; but to no avail. That night, taking with him only a few books, he leaves for the convent of St. Augustine. Asking admittance, he is received, and the talented young doctor is separated from the world. Only twenty-two, and shut away from his parents and all that he loves best on earth!

> Dying souls, fast bound in sin,
>   Trembling and repining;
> With no ray of light Divine
>   On your pathway shining;
> Why in darkness wander on,
>   Filled with consternation?
> Jesus lives—in Him alone
>   Can you find salvation.

THE MONK

Chapter 3

THE MONK

In Him was life; and the life was the light of men.—John 1:4.

JOHN LUTHER was very angry when he heard what his son had done. All the bright hopes that he had cherished seemed overthrown. It was not until two of his other sons died of the plague, and he heard it reported that Martin was dead also, that he forgave him. The friends at Erfurt were astonished. For two days they clustered round the convent, hoping to see Luther; but the gates remained closed and barred. A month passed away before they were able to speak to their former companion.

When Martin Luther entered the convent, he changed his name, and took that of Augustine.

What is the young monk doing? Is he full of joy because his sins are gone? No; sin is still there. Is he happy in his studies? No; he must work, not read. The monks at first treat him very harshly. He is made the porter, to open and shut the gates; he has to wind the clock, sweep the church, and clean the cells. When this is done, he takes his bag and begs from house to house. He returns tired, and thinks now he will be able to rest and read his books, but the other monks come and roughly call him away, saying: "Come, come! it is not by studying, but by begging bread, corn, eggs, fish, meat, and money that a monk renders himself useful to the cloister."

He bears all patiently, thinking these unpleasant things are but discipline leading to holiness. At the intercession of the University he is after a time, freed from his meaner duties, and returns to his studies. But his studies, his fasting, his sleepless nights, wear him away, and he becomes pale and thin. His mind is still vigorous, and frequently he may be seen in public debate unraveling the most complicated reasoning.

In the convent he had found a Bible fastened by a chain. To this he constantly returns. He loves the Word of God, but as yet it speaks to him only of that holiness which he cannot attain. He tries more earnestly, he shuts himself up in his cell, repeats his Latin prayers over and over. But his conscience troubles him, and he says to himself: "Look, thou art still envious, impatient, passionate. It profiteth thee nothing. Oh! wretched man, to have entered this sacred order!" For seven weeks he has hardly slept; for four days he has remained without eating or drinking. On one occasion he shut himself up in his cell, and suffered no one to enter for several days. A friend, named Lucas Edemberger, feeling anxious about him, took with him chorister boys, and knocked at his door. No one opens, no one answers—all is still! Much alarmed, Edemberger breaks open the door.

The Monk

Luther lies upon the floor apparently dead. He is worn out with fasting, want of sleep, and unhappiness of heart. His friend strives in vain to bring him to his senses, and it is only when he hears the sweet voices of the boys singing a hymn that he returns to consciousness. His troubles caused him more attentively to study the Bible, and the time is now drawing near when he is to meet with a friend to whom he can tell all his sorrows.

John Staupitz, the vicar-general of the Augustine convents in Germany, was about to visit Erfurt. He was a good man, who knew much of the love and mercy of Jesus, and had a kind heart. He himself had endured similar struggles to those of Luther, and had found peace in Jesus Christ. As he was making his usual inspection of the convent at Erfurt, and the monks were gathered before him, he especially noticed one—a young man of middle height, whom study, fasting, and prolonged watchings had wasted away till all his bones could be counted. This young man was Luther. Staupitz, quickly seeing what was passing within, very kindly approached him, and succeeded in gaining his confidence. He showed him how useless it was to trust in good works for salvation, and explained the way in which God pardons sin through faith in Jesus; he also told him how foolish it was to wait for repentance before he believed in the loving kindness of God. "If you desire to be converted," said he, "do not be anxious about these mortifications, and all these tortures. Love Him who first loved you!" Staupitz did more than this; for, on leaving the convent, he gave Luther a Bible, and encouraged him to let the study of the Scriptures be his favorite occupation.

Never was advice better taken and obeyed. The dark clouds were now rolling away. Happiness began to dawn upon the young monk; but the mists had not quite dispersed. The good seed had been sown in his heart, but there yet remained much for him to learn.

He was again laid aside by sickness, and appeared to be dying. His anxieties and fears returned, and he was sinking into despair. An old monk entered his cell, and spoke kindly to him. Luther told him of his misery and fear. The old man could not counsel like Staupitz, but he knew his creed, and it had comforted his heart. Simply he repeated, "I believe in the forgiveness of sins." The sick man slowly said the words, "I believe in the forgiveness of sins." "Ah!" exclaimed the aged brother, "you must believe not only in the forgiveness of David's and Peter's sins, but you must believe that your own sins are forgiven." "Hear also what St. Bernard says," said he: " 'The testimony in thy heart is this: thy sins are forgiven thee.' "

From this moment Luther had peace, and could say with St. Paul, "Being justified by faith, we have peace with God through our Lord Jesus Christ." He realized also the power of the Saviour's words, "Peace I leave with you; my peace I give unto you: not as the world giveth, give I unto you."

The Monk

Jesus, Thou art my righteousness,
  For all my sins were Thine;
Thy death hath bought of God my peace
  Thy life hath made Him mine.
Spotless and just in Thee I am;
  I feel my sins forgiven:
I taste salvation in Thy name,
  And antedate my heaven.

LUTHER AT WITTENBERG

Chapter 4

LUTHER AT WITTENBERG

With joy shall ye draw water out of the wells of salvation.—Isa. 12:3.

LUTHER HAD BEEN A MONK nearly two years when, on May 2, 1507, he was ordained a priest. He had invited his father to be present at the ceremony, and had asked him to choose the day. John Luther accepted the invitation, and showed his affection and generosity by presenting the young priest with twenty florins.

After the ordination, John dined at the convent with his son and the other Augustine monks. The conversation turned to the subject of Luther's entering the monastery. The monks praised him greatly for so doing; but the father, turning to his son, said, "Have you not read in Scripture that you should obey your father and mother?" These words sank deeply into Luther's heart.

New scenes were now about to open before the young priest, and a different, but more congenial position was to be assigned to him.

Staupitz, who had not forgotten the young monk, but corresponded frequently with him, spoke of him to Frederick, the good and wise Elector of Saxony, who invited him to become professor at the University of Wittenberg. This was in 1508.

Upon his arrival at Wittenberg he went to the Augustine convent, where a cell was prepared for him; for though now a professor, he still remained a monk. He zealously entered upon his new duties, and was appointed to teach a great many learned and difficult subjects. But his desire was for the Bible— for time to study it himself, and for opportunity to teach it to others. He continued the study of Greek and Hebrew, so that he might be able to read the Scriptures in their original languages. A few months after this, having obtained the degree of Bachelor of Divinity, he was called upon to lecture on the Bible every day at one o'clock.

Luther was now engaged in a work that he loved. The Word of God became more and more precious to him, and he delighted to impart its truths to his pupils. While studying for one of his lectures a bright light seemed to shine upon Romans 1:7, "The just shall live by faith." This text had a great influence in molding the character of the reformer.

Staupitz rejoiced in the talents of his friend, and, wishing him to be still more useful, asked him to preach in the Church of the Augustines. "No, no!" he replied, "it is no slight thing to speak before men in the place of God." Staupitz persevered, and at last Luther yielded.

In the middle of the Square at Wittenberg stood an old wooden chapel, thirty feet long and twenty wide.

Its walls were propped up on all sides, and an old pulpit, made of planks, three feet high, received the preacher. In this humble place the preaching of the Reformation began.

The minds of the people at this time were not enlightened. God's Word was unknown. Ignorance and superstition prevailed. They worshiped old bones, which they were told had been parts of the bodies of holy men, bits of wood, and other relics. They heard prayers in Latin, and bowed down at the mass. If they did wrong they went to a priest, confessed, and did penance; or procured an indulgence. They believed in a dreadful purgatory, in whose flames the souls of the departed must be tortured until satisfaction had been made for their crimes. The bishops and priests were too often bad men, who gained money by picturing the dreadful sufferings of those in purgatory, telling the people that if they paid money the tortured souls of those they loved would be liberated sooner. Truly darkness covered the land, and gross darkness the people.

Luther preached. He was still a Papist, but he was drawing truth from the Bible. Everything about the new minister was striking. His clear voice, his noble air, his expressive countenance, charmed his hearers; while the deep seriousness of his manner, and the joy that evidently filled his heart, when he spoke of the love of Christ for sinners, gave to his eloquence authority and warmth which deeply impressed his hearers.

His fame spread far and wide, the little chapel

could not contain the crowds that flocked to it, and Luther was asked to preach in the parish church. Frederick the Elector once came to Wittenberg to hear him.

> In a service which Thy love appoints,
>   There are no bonds for me:
> For my secret heart is taught the truth
>   That makes Thy people free;
> And a life of self-renouncing love,
>   Is a life of liberty.

THE VISIT TO ROME

Chapter 5

THE VISIT TO ROME

Having a form of godliness, but denying the power thereof: from such turn away.—II Tim. 3:5.

LUTHER IMAGINED Rome to be a most holy city. It was necessary for him to see it, and he visited it in 1510.

There was a difference of opinion between Staupitz and seven of the Augustine convents, and Luther was chosen to lay the matter before the Pope.

He set out, crossed the Alps and descended into the plains of Italy. At every step he found subjects of astonishment and scandal. He was entertained in a wealthy Italian convent of the Benedictines. When he saw the splendid apartments, the rich dresses, and the delicate food, he was confounded. Marble, silk, luxury in all its forms—what a sight for the humble brother of the poor convent of Wittenberg! Friday came—a fast day with Roman Catholics—but Luther saw the table with meat. He was shocked, and resolved to speak. "The Church and the Pope," he said, "forbid such things." The Benedictines were very angry, and the porter of the convent warned him that it would be dangerous to stay longer. He left this wealthy convent and went on to Bologna, where he became dangerously ill.

Recovered from his sickness, he proceeded on, and, after a toilsome journey under a burning Italian sun, he saw at length the seven-hilled city in the distance. Falling on his knees, he exclaimed: "Holy Rome, I salute thee!" But when he entered the city and saw the great wickedness on every hand, he felt that it was far from holy. He saw that the priests and high dignitaries of the Church made a mock of religion, or else performed their duties with haste and in a mechanical manner. On one occasion he was engaged in celebrating mass, when he found that the priests at an adjoining altar had repeated seven masses before he had finished one. Growing impatient, a priest cried out to him, "Make haste, make haste; have done with it quickly."

Luther went to Rome a devout Papist, and at first gave himself up to all the superstitions of the Church. He visited the churches and chapels, he believed the falsehoods that were told him, he knelt before the shrines of the saints—he even wished that his parents were dead, so that by his good works he might have the pleasure of delivering their souls from purgatory. One day, wishing to obtain an indulgence, which the Pope had promised to all who should ascend on their knees what is called Pilate's Staircase, he began slowly to crawl up those steps, when a voice like thunder seemed to speak from the bottom of his heart, "The just shall live by faith." He started from his knees,

The Visit to Rome

and rushed from the spot ashamed of his superstitious folly.

Luther went to Rome, believing that city to be the holiest spot upon earth; he left it with the conviction, expressed in his own words: "No one can imagine what sins and infamous actions are committed in Rome; they must be seen and heard to be believed. Thus they are in the habit of saying, 'If there be a hell, Rome is built over it'; it is an abyss whence issues every kind of sin."

This visit was of great importance to Luther, and he afterward said, "If they would give me one hundred thousand florins I would not have missed seeing Rome."

Having finished the business entrusted to him, he returned to Wittenberg.

The preaching of the young professor had made a deep impression on the Elector, and that prince, and also Staupitz, wished to advance him to yet higher honors. He was therefore made Doctor of Divinity, the Elector generously agreeing to pay all expenses. This was on October 19, 1512. He then solemnly promised to preach the Holy Scriptures faithfully, to teach them with purity, to study them all his life, and to defend them, both orally and in writing, against all false teachers, so far as God should give him ability.

Nobly Luther kept his vow, and not only in the University classes, and in the church, did he preach the gospel, but among private friends he was always anxious to lead them to trust in Jesus and Him crucified.

About this time he became acquainted with George Spalatin, secretary and chaplain to the Elector, a man of great worth, to whom Luther became much attached. Through his hands passed all the business between the reformer and the Elector.

In 1516, Staupitz was sent by Frederick into the Low Countries to collect relics; and Luther was appointed to take his place during his absence, and in particular to visit the convents in his stead.

Among others, he came to the monastery at Erfurt where he had once wound the clock, opened the gates, and swept the church. He was now visiting it as the vicar-general, and we know that he tried to comfort many hearts. He urged the monks to lay aside their books of philosophy and to study the Word of God. Many of the Augustine monks afterward became faithful preachers of the gospel, and so much good followed from this journey that the year in which it took place has been called "the morning star of the Reformation." He returned to Wittenberg after an absence of about six weeks.

About this time the plague broke out in that town. Many fled, but Luther remained. "You advise me to flee," he wrote to a friend: "whither shall I flee? If the pestilence spreads, I shall disperse the brothers in every direction; but as for me, my place is here; duty does not permit me to desert my post until He who has called me shall summon me away. Not that

The Visit to Rome

I have no fear of death, but I hope that the Lord will deliver me from fear."

Such was the brave and faithful man who was to attack the giant power of Rome with the sword of the Spirit, the Word of God. As yet, he was full of respect for the Pope and the Romish religion.

Staupitz returned with a valuable supply of relics, and the Elector, greatly pleased, thought to make him a bishop. Luther, who was bold in the presence of the terrible plague, was also bold before the mighty of this world. He wrote to Spalatin telling him that it was wrong, and saying: "There are many things which please your prince, and which nevertheless are displeasing to God."

In July, 1517, he preached before Duke George of Saxony, in whose States Dresden and Leipsic were situated. The sermon gave great offense to the Duke and his Court, but was made a blessing to a lady of high rank, who, a month afterward, died trusting in Jesus.

> O Christ! He is the fountain,
>   The deep, sweet well of love;
> The streams on earth I've tasted,
>   More deep I'll drink above;
> There to an ocean fulness,
>   His mercy doth expand,
> And glory—glory dwelleth
>   In Emmanuel's land.

THE INDULGENCES

Chapter 6

THE INDULGENCES

I, even I, am He that blotteth out thy transgressions for mine own sake, and will not remember thy sins.—Isa. 43:25.

A GREAT AGITATION now prevailed in Germany. Pope Leo X wanted money to meet the lavish expenditure of his Court and the expense incurred by the building of St. Peter's Church. He issued a bull, or edict, declaring a general indulgence—to be paid for by those who received it—the proceeds of which were to be appropriated to the building of St. Peter's.

The sale of these indulgences caused great scandal in Germany. The sins of the Germans, as they were called, had been delegated to Albert, the Archbishop and Elector of Mentz; and the agent employed by him was a Dominican monk, John Tetzel, a bad man, whom the Emperor Maximilian, on one occasion, ordered to be put into a sack and thrown into the river on account of his crimes.

Tetzel was forbidden to enter the dominions of Frederick the Elector; he came as near as he could,

45

and established himself at Juterbuch, four miles from Wittenberg.

A grand procession is advancing! In clouds of dust a handsome carriage approaches, accompanied by three horsemen. Instantly the whole town is astir. The clergy, priests and nuns, carrying lighted tapers; the council; the schoolmasters and their pupils; the tradesmen with their banners; men and women, young and old, all go out to meet the company. With music playing and bells ringing, they follow it to the church.

The Pope's bull is carried on a velvet cushion, or on cloth of gold, in front of the procession. Next follows Tetzel, robed in a Dominican's dress, moving along with an arrogant air, and bearing in his hands a large red cross. Others follow.

When they arrive at the church, the cross is placed in front of the altar, the Pope's insignia is hung upon it, and daily the clergy of the place and others come to pay it homage.

The church is crowded, the large red cross stands before the altar. Tetzel—a strong man of sixty-three—is in the pulpit. He has come to sell God's pardon for sin. In a loud voice he begins to extol his wares. "Indulgences," he says, "are the most precious of God's gifts. Come, and I will give you letters, all properly sealed, by which even the sins that you intend to commit may be pardoned. There is no sin so great that an indulgence cannot remit; only pay well, and all will be forgiven." He passes to another subject. "But more than this," he says, "indulgences

The Indulgences

avail not only for the living, but for the dead. For that, repentance is not even necessary. Priest, noble, merchant, wife, youth, maiden! do you not hear your parents and your friends who are dead crying out to you: 'We are suffering horrible torments; a little money will deliver us; you can give it, and you will not!'" All shuddered at the words, uttered by the thundering voice of the imposter monk. "At the very instant that the money rattles at the bottom of the chest, the soul escapes from purgatory, and flies liberated to heaven."

There was a money-box near, and as the monk spoke, people dropped in their coins. His speech ended, he ran toward the box, and in the sight of all flung in a piece of money, taking care that it should rattle loudly. And now the sale began; crowds came with their money to buy the indulgences which assured them of the pardon of their sins, and of permission to sin again.

How awful it was for any man to offer to sell for money that pardon which Jesus Christ purchased by His blood; or to give permission to sin, when God says, "The soul that sinneth it shall die"!

Tetzel had a regular price for different sins. To the poor his charge for murder was eight ducats, while for sacrilege and perjury he charged nine.

With all his cunning, sometimes Tetzel was taken in. On one occasion a Saxon nobleman, who had heard him at Leipsic, and was much displeased with his falsehoods, came and asked him if he had the power of pardoning sins that men intended to commit. "Most assuredly," he replied. "I have received full power from His Holiness for that purpose." "Well, then," answered the knight, "I am desirous of taking a slight revenge on one of my enemies, without endangering his life. I will give you ten crowns if you will give me a letter of indulgence that will fully justify me." Tetzel made some objection, but they came to an arrangement for thirty crowns. The monk left Leipsic shortly after. The nobleman and his attendants watched for him in a wood. They fell upon him and gave him a slight beating, taking from him the well-filled indulgence chest which he was carrying. Tetzel was in a furious rage; but the nobleman showed the letter of indulgence, and Duke George ordered him to be acquitted.

One upon whom Tetzel's proceedings made the deepest impression was the youthful Myconius, afterward celebrated as a reformer and historian of the Reformation.

Luther appears to have first heard of Tetzel at Grimma in 1516. Hearing some of his extravagant expressions quoted, he said, "If God permit, I will make a hole in his drum."

One day Luther, as a priest, was hearing his people confess their sins. Many acknowledged themselves guilty of great crimes. He rebuked them, and tried to make them lead better lives; but he was shocked and indignant when they replied that they would not abandon their sins, and that they need not, for they had bought indulgences of Tetzel. He refused to absolve them, and said, "Except ye repent, ye shall all

The Indulgences

likewise perish." Then he added, "Have a care how you listen to the clamors of these indulgence merchants; you have better things to do than buy their licenses which they sell at so vile a price."

When Tetzel heard of this he bellowed with rage, and had a fire lighted in the market place, declaring that he had received an order from the Pope to burn all heretics who presumed to oppose his holy indulgences.

Luther, nothing daunted, ascended the pulpit of his church and preached boldly against them. This he did notwithstanding that special indulgences had been granted by the Pope for the Elector's castle-chapel at Wittenberg.

The sermon was printed, and made a profound impression on all who read it.

> My hope is built on nothing less
> Than Jesus' blood and righteousness;
> I dare not trust the sweetest frame,
> But wholly lean on Jesus' name;
> On Christ the solid rock I stand;
> All other ground is sinking sand.

THE THESES

Chapter 7

THE THESES

Who can forgive sins, but God alone?—Luke 5:21.

LUTHER PREPARED for a yet bolder step. He had warned his people in the confessional, he had preached from the pulpit to his congregation; he would now speak as a theologian, addressing all those who, like himself, were teachers of the Word of God. The feast of All Saints drew near, a very important day at Wittenberg, especially for the church which Frederick had built and filled with relics. On this day these relics, ornamented with gold, silver, and precious stones, were exhibited to the people, and whoever then visited the church, and made confession, obtained a rich indulgence.

On the day preceding the festival, October 31, 1517, Luther walked boldly toward the church, and in the presence of all who were assembled, posted on the church door a paper containing ninety-five short sentences, called theses, against the doctrine of indulgences. Three of them were:

> "They preach mere human follies who maintain that as soon as the money rattles in the strong box the soul flies out of purgatory."

"They are the enemies of the Pope and of Jesus Christ, who, by reason of the preaching of indulgences, forbid the preaching of the Word of God."

"The indulgence of the Pope cannot take away the smallest daily sin, as far as regards the guilt or the offense."

Great was the attention excited. The Theses were read and spoken of on all sides. In a fortnight they were in every part of Germany, and in a month they had found their way to Rome. Somewhat later they were translated into Dutch and Spanish, and a traveler sold them in Jerusalem. Many were delighted with them; monks in their cells and peasants in their cottages rejoiced that they had heard the voice of truth. The Emperor Maximilian read them, and wrote to the Elector of Saxony, "Take great care of the monk Luther, for the time may come when we shall have need of him." Even the Pope was more amused than angry, and when urged to burn him as a heretic, replied, "Brother Martin Luther is a very fine genius, and all that is said against him is mere monkish jealousy."

But some were fearful of the results that would follow. The Elector was uneasy, and the principal men of Luther's own convent were alarmed. They came to his cell trembling, and begged him not to bring disgrace upon their order. He nobly replied, "Dear fathers, if this work be not of God, it will come to nought; but if it be, let it go forward."

Tetzel prepared some theses in reply to those of

Luther. Not content with this, he stated his hope and belief that the heretic would be burned. As a sign he caused the reformer's Theses to be cast into the flames—an act which was afterward repaid by the students of Wittenberg, who burned his own theses in the market place of that town.

Luther was much grieved when he heard of this revenge having been taken. He wished for peace and order, and always maintained that the cause of God was not to be advanced by any recourse to force or arms.

About this time he published his sermons on the Ten Commandments and his *Explanation of the Lord's Prayer.* These works were issued with the object of carrying the truth to the homes of the people.

The contest continued. The Dominicans were especially fierce in their assault. The Bishop of Brandenburg said, "I will not lay my head down in peace until I have thrown Martin into the fire like this brand," (he threw a piece of wood into the fire). But the most violent in his attack was one who had been a friend, Dr. Eck, of Ingolstadt. Luther wrote him a letter of affection, but to this he received no reply. Rome now began to take part in the combat; Prierio, the Roman censor, attacked the reformer's Theses, employing by turns ridicule, insults, and menaces.

In the spring of 1518, Luther was called to take part in an important meeting of the Augustine order, held at Heidelberg. Here he so ably defended some theses which he had written that he won much applause. Better still, he was the means of bringing many to see the light—one of whom was Bucer, who afterward wrote many good books which were made a great blessing to England.

On his return from Heidelberg, Luther wrote an explanation of his Theses, firmly upholding the truth, but softening down some passages that had given offense. He sent this book, which he called *"Resolutions,"* to the Pope through his friend Staupitz, with a letter full of humility, respect, and submission.

Luther wished for peace, and supposed that Leo X was a just man and a sincere lover of the truth. In this we shall see that he was mistaken.

But while he was looking to the Pope for justice, Rome was planning vengeance against him. The first effort made was to draw away the powerful support of the Elector, but this failed. The next step was to cite him to Rome. The Emperor Maximilian had written a letter to the Pope concerning the reformer, in which he said, "We will take care that whatever your Holiness may decree in this matter, for the glory of God shall be enforced throughout the empire;" and Leo X began to consider it was time to put forth his strength and to crush the poor Augustine monk who had dared to preach against his indulgences.

Having sent his letter to the Pope, Luther left the matter in the hands of God, and quietly awaited the result. Only two days had elapsed, however, when he received a summons to appear at Rome to answer charges made against him.

"At the very moment I was expecting a blessing," he said, "I saw the thunderbolt fall upon me. I was the lamb that troubled the water the wolf was drinking. Tetzel escaped, and I was to permit myself to be devoured."

His friends were filled with alarm. If he went to Rome, he went, as they saw, to certain death, while if he refused to appear he would be condemned for disrespect of the Pope's authority. Luther felt that only the Elector could save him, but he was unwilling to involve his kind prince in trouble. The University of Wittenberg wrote a letter of entreaty to the Pope, and also to his chamberlain, Charles Miltitz. They said, "The weakness of Luther's frame and the dangers of the journey render it difficult, and even impossible, for him to obey the order of your Holiness." The Elector also wrote to the Emperor concerning him.

Finally it was arranged that the reformer should appear in Augsburg, a German city, instead of at Rome; and the Pope ordered his legate, Cardinal Cajetan—otherwise known as De Vio—to try the matter there. This was not done by the Pope out of any compassion for Luther. His writ was cruel, and authorized the legate to prosecute the Wittenberg doctor without delay, to invoke the aid of the Emperor and princes of Germany, to keep the reformer in safe custody, and to excommunicate all those who adhered to his cause. He was proceeded against by the Bishop of Ascoli, and declared a heretic, unheard.

Luther was at this time much cheered by the arrival at Wittenberg of a young man of great ability and much gentleness. It was Philip Melancthon, who became a very dear friend, and was destined to take a leading part with him in the work of the Reformation. Melancthon had been invited by the Elector to become professor of ancient languages at the University of Wittenberg. He was then twenty-one years of age.

The Pope wrote a very flattering letter to the Elector, in which he urged him to watch over the honor of his name, and to deliver Luther into the legate's hands. The good Elector did not yield, but sent him letters of recommendation to some of the principal councilors of Augsburg, and furnished him with money for his journey.

The citation to Rome having been changed to a summons to appear at Augsburg, Luther resolved to obey it, although entreated by many of his friends not to do so, and informed that several powerful lords had determined to strangle or drown him on his way. Staupitz was much alarmed, and wrote begging Martin to come and live with him, so that both might live and die together.

But Luther feared nothing but sinning against God. The words of Scripture continually sounded in his ears, "Whosoever shall confess me before men, him will I also confess before my father which is in heaven."

> Soon, and for ever! the work shall be done,
> The warfare accomplished, the victory won;
> Soon, and for ever! the soldier lay down

His sword for a harp, and his cross for a crown;
Then droop not in sorrow, despond not in fear,
A glorious tomorrow is brightening and near.

AUGSBURG

Chapter 8

AUGSBURG

Our soul is escaped as a bird out of the snare of the fowlers: the snare is broken, and we are escaped.—Ps. 124:7.

WE HAVE SEEN LUTHER contending with Tetzel, we have witnessed him defending his Theses in the presence of learned doctors; we are now about to see him brought face to face with the power of Rome itself.

Having received the letters of recommendation sent him by the Elector, he quietly set out on foot for Augsburg. He must have felt sad as he left his much-loved Wittenberg to appear before the Roman legate, and without a guarantee of safe conduct. Death may be very near, but he advanced without fear to bear his testimony to the gospel.

On September 28 he reached Weimar, where the Elector was holding his Court. Here he preached. He next stopped at Nuremberg, where, as his own was old, he borrowed a frock from his friend Wenceslas Link, the preacher there, so that he might appear in becoming dress before the prince of the Roman

Church. From this town, Link and a monk named Leonard accompanied him.

When within five leagues of Augsburg, Luther was taken so ill that he thought he was going to die. His friends procured a wagon, in which they placed him, and in this condition he entered the city on Friday, October 7, 1518.

He took up his abode at the convent of the Augustines, where he recovered.

His first business was to send Link to the Cardinal to announce his arrival.

The next morning, while thinking upon his peculiar position, he was informed that a stranger was about to visit him. Shortly after, a cunning Italian courtier, Serra Longa, appeared, and in a most plausible manner tried to get Luther to retract. He came as a friend, but he was sent as a spy by the Cardinal. Failing in this, he went away. Meanwhile the councilors, to whom the Elector had recommended Luther, strongly urged him not to go before the legate without safe conduct, which they offered to procure.

Serra Longa returned, and stated that the Cardinal was waiting. Luther informed him of the advice of his Augsburg friends, and refused to proceed until safe conduct arrived.

In acting thus, Luther well knew that safe conduct had not saved John Huss from being burned. He only insisted upon having one in compliance with the wishes of those to whom the Elector had entrusted him.

On the Monday following, the safe-conduct ar-

Augsburg

rived, and Cajetan was informed that Luther would wait upon him on the morrow.

Shortly before the arrival of the safe-conduct, Serra Longa again appeared. "Why do you not wait upon the Cardinal?" he said. "He is expecting you most indulgently. The whole matter lies in six letters—*r-e-v-o-c-a*—retract. Come, you have nothing to fear." Luther thought these six letters very important ones, but he told him that he was waiting for safe-conduct, when he would immediately appear before Cajetan.

Serra Longa grew very angry, and, after accusing Luther of imagining that the Elector would take up arms in his defense, said, "When all forsake you, where will you take refuge?"

Luther looking upward said, "Under Heaven."

Serra Longa added, "What would you do if you held the legate, Pope, and cardinals in your hands, as they have you now in theirs?"

Luther answered, "I would show them all possible honor and respect, but with me the Word of God is before everything."

Such was the sturdy man whom Rome thought to conquer. His strength was in the Lord of Hosts, and his weapon the Sword of the Spirit—the Word of God.

Accompanied by a few friends, Luther, on Tuesday, October 11 went to the palace of the legate. Crowds pressed upon him as he went along. Cajetan received him with coldness but civility. When the salutations were over, Luther stated that he appeared in obedience to the summons of the Pope and the orders of the Elector of Saxony. He acknowledged the propositions and theses ascribed to him. He was ready to listen to his accusation, and, if he had erred, to receive instruction in the truth.

But Cajetan had not received instructions to argue with the reformer. At first he spoke kindly, saying, "My dear son." Pointing out two propositions, he requested Luther retract them. Finding him firm, he grew angry, and said, "I did not come here to dispute with you. Retract, or prepare to suffer the penalty you have deserved."

Having refused a safe-conduct to appear at Rome, the reformer withdrew.

A very pleasant surprise awaited him upon his arrival at the convent. His old friend Staupitz, unable to prevent his appearance at Augsburg, had journeyed thither to offer him his services in this time of trial. Great was Luther's joy when he saw his friend.

On the advice of Staupitz, the reformer determined to answer the Cardinal in writing.

Accordingly, taking with him a notary public, he returned to the legate's palace the next day, and in the presence of all assembled read the declaration which he had prepared. He stated his willingness to receive instruction, but protested against being compelled to retract without having been refuted.

Cajetan would hear nothing but the words, "I retract." Turning to the two propositions, he overwhelmed Luther with objections, allowing him no opportunity of replying.

Luther, and Staupitz, who had accompanied him, saw the hopelessness of attempting either to enlighten the Cardinal or to make any useful confession of faith. The reformer begged leave to transmit his answer in writing. This request, being supported by his friends, was granted. The second interview had ended as unsatisfactorily as the first.

On Friday, the 14th, he returned to the Cardinal for the third and last time. The Italians, who formed the train of this prince of the Church, crowded around him as usual. He advanced and presented the protest that he had written. Cajetan glanced at it, and threw the paper aside with contempt, declaring that Luther ought to retract. The interview ended in threatenings. The legate, having been confounded upon a point on which he laid special stress, cried out, "Retract! retract! or, if you do not, I shall send you to Rome. I shall excommunicate you with all your partisans, with all who are or may be favorable to you, and reject them from the Church."

"Deign," replied Luther, "to forward to Pope Leo X, with my humble prayers, the answer which I have handed you in writing."

Cajetan answered with pride and anger, "Retract, or return no more."

Luther took account of the words and withdrew. He and Cajetan never met again, but the reformer had made an impression on the legate which was never entirely effaced.

Later in the day the Cardinal sent for Staupitz and Wenceslas Link, urged them to persuade Luther to retract; but this they declared was beyond their power. He then stated that he would send to the reformer, in writing, what he should retract.

Saturday and Sunday passed without any writing coming from Cajetan. Luther's friends began to be much alarmed. "The legate," said they, "is preparing some mischief, and it is very much to be feared that all of you will be seized and cast into prison."

On Monday, Luther wrote to the Cardinal, but received no reply. Fearing this stillness on the part of the legate and his courtiers boded no good. Those to whom the reformer had been confided urged him to draw up an appeal to the Pope, and to quit Augsburg without delay. Staupitz, Link, and the Elector's councilors had already left.

Having waited four days in the city uselessly, he determined to leave. Before doing so he wrote a second letter to the Cardinal, which was to be given to that prelate after the reformer's departure. He also drew up an appeal to the Pope, to be posted upon the cathedral gates two or three days after he had left.

On Wednesday, before daylight, a pony which Staupitz had left for him was brought to the door of the convent. Luther bade his brethren farewell. Without a bridle for his horse, without boots or spurs, and unarmed, he set off. A guide had been provided who conducted him in silence through the streets. They had made their way to a small wall-gate of the city, which had purposely been left open. They passed through, and soon the poor but nobleminded monk, who had dared to oppose the haughty power of Rome, galloped away far from the walls of Augsburg.

> When exposed to fearful dangers,
> Jesus will his own defend;
> Borne afar, midst foes and strangers,
> Jesus will appear your Friend;
> And His presence
> Shall be with you to the end.

A TRUCE

Chapter 9

A TRUCE

Behold, God is my salvation; I will trust, and not be afraid.—Isa. 12:2.

CAJETAN WAS EXCEEDINGLY MORTIFIED when he heard of Luther's escape. He was thunderstruck, even frightened and alarmed. He had done nothing; he had neither humbled Luther nor punished him. He wrote a letter to the Elector desiring that prince either to send the reformer to Rome, or to banish him from his dominions; adding a postscript in his own writing entreating Frederick "not to tarnish his honor and that of his illustrious ancestors for the sake of a miserable friar."

The Elector refused either to send Luther to Rome or to banish him from his States. Although secure in the Elector's favor, Luther felt that he might be compelled to leave Germany. He looked to France as the country where he might hope to have the opportunity of announcing the truth without fear of opposition.

The hour of his departure indeed seemed at hand. He had written to the Elector begging that he might not be sent to Rome, but offering to resign himself to banishment. He had preached a farewell sermon to his congregation, and now he waited in humble trust the will of Him without whose knowledge not a sparrow falls to the ground.

The prince informed Luther that he desired him to leave Wittenberg. A farewell repast was provided. His friends once more gathered around him. He enjoyed their sweet conversation, their tender and anxious friendship. A knock came; a letter arrived! The Elector inquired why he delayed so long. He was sad, but a bright ray of comfort came. He lifted up his head and joyfully exclaimed, as he looked on those around him, "Father and mother abandon me, but the Lord takes me up." Tears rolled down the cheeks of his friends. Another messenger; a second letter from the Elector! Everything was changed. "Since the Pope's new envoy hopes that all may be arranged by a conference, remain for the present."

Luther now published his report of the Augsburg Conference. On November 28, 1518, in the chapel of Corpus Christi at Wittenberg, he appealed from the Pope to a General Council of the Church. This was a bold step. A former Pope had pronounced the greater excommunication even against the emperors who should be guilty of such an act of revolt.

An event now happened which partly diverted the attention of the Pope from the German reformer. On January 12, 1519, the Emperor Maximilian of Germany died, and Frederick of Saxony became the administrator of the empire. He was, therefore, enabled more powerfully to protect Luther, and to disregard the projects of papal nuncios.

A Truce

The Pope was also so much engaged in his plans concerning the election of a new emperor, that the contest about indulgences seemed of comparatively small importance.

The new papal nuncio, Charles Miltitz, arrived in Saxony about this time. Having been informed of the scandalous proceedings of Tetzel, he became very angry, summoned that monk before him, and, upon his refusing to appear, went to Dresden where he was, and so overwhelmed him with reproaches that he was driven to despair, and soon afterward died. Before his death, Luther, who pitied his old and bitter enemy, wrote him a letter full of kindness and consolation.

Miltitz thought that Cajetan had been too hasty in dealing with Luther, and therefore he tried flattery. They met in the house of Spalatin at Altenburg. "Do you know," said Miltitz, addressing the reformer, "that you have drawn away all the world from the Pope; even if I had an army of 25,000 men I do not think that I should be able to carry you to Rome." He had with him seventy briefs to be used for carrying him thither if the Elector delivered the reformer into his hands.

After preparing the way, as he thought, he cautiously hinted at a retractation; but Luther was determined not to retract unless it was proved that he was in error. He acknowledged that he might have spoken too violently sometimes. "But," he said, "as for a retractation, never expect one from me."

At the close of the conference, a truce was signed,

both parties agreeing that they would in the future neither preach, write, nor do anything further in the discussion that had been raised.

Luther was at this time full of respect for the Church of Rome, and, in his desire for peace, went so far as to write a letter to the Pope, concluding with these words: "I confess that nothing in Heaven or in earth should be preferred above the Church of Rome, except Jesus Christ alone, the Lord of all."

Strange words to our ears; but in Luther's case light slowly came out of darkness. He afterward affirmed that "it is not necessary to salvation that we should believe the Roman Church superior to others."

During the pause which now ensued in the strife, the reformer employed himself in studying the decretals of the Popes. The work of the Reformation also progressed, and the writings of the Wittenberg professor were scattered over France, the Low Countries, Italy, Spain, England, and Switzerland, everywhere creating the greatest sensation. The truce agreed to was soon broken, however, and the combat was renewed.

Dr. Eck commenced the strife, and the famous Leipsic discussion, which lasted seventeen days, was the immediate cause of setting in motion those powers which had for a short space lain dormant.

This disputation dealt with the free will of man, the supremacy of the Pope, the doctrines of indulgences, purgatory, repentance, absolution of the priest, and satisfaction. Eck, one of the most experi-

A Truce

enced schoolmen of his age, was a formidable opponent; but truth was on the side of Luther. The Catholic theologian had to resort to subtle and fallacious reasoning to meet the powerful arguments the reformer drew from the Word of God.

Luther thought that much time had been wasted without any seeking after truth; but good had been done. The truth had sunk into some hearts. Dr. Eck's secretary, Poliander; John Callarius, a celebrated Hebrew professor; and Philip Melancthon, the theologian of the Reformation, dated their conversion from this period. Luther himself was brought to see the utter fallacy of the papal pretensions to supremacy.

From this time Eck became the reformer's bitterest enemy; and early in the following year 1520, he set out for Rome, intending to rouse the papacy to crush his powerful rival.

Luther continued to advance. About this time he published his first Commentary on Galatians. He also questioned the authority of the Popes to canonize saints, and was led to see that the Lord's Supper was not present in the mass (the mass was not a true observance of the Lord's Supper).

> He leadeth me, oh blessed thought!
> O words with heavenly comfort fraught:
> Whate'er I do, where'er I be,
> Still 'tis God's hand that leadeth me.

THE PAPAL BULL

Chapter 10

THE PAPAL BULL

Be strong and of a good courage, fear not, nor be afraid of them: for the Lord thy God, He it is that doth go with thee; He will not fail thee, nor forsake thee.—Deut. 31:6.

WHEN THE YEAR 1520 OPENED, Maximilian was dead, and a new emperor had to be chosen.

The imperial crown had been offered to the Elector Frederick, but that prince in his modesty declined it. The election fell upon Charles, who already possessed sovereign authority over the two Spains, Naples, Sicily, and Austria. As Charles V he was crowned Emperor of Germany, with unusual pomp and magnificence, at Aix-la-Chapelle. The date was October 22, 1520.

Luther, seeing that the cause of the Reformation would soon be carried before the new emperor, wrote to him before he left Madrid; but the young monarch took no notice of his letter.

His life was now in great danger. Fanaticism was kindled in Germany. Now is the time," he wrote, "when men will think they do Christ service by putting us to death." One day as he was in front of the

Augustine convent, a stranger, who held a pistol concealed under his cloak, accosted him: "Why do you go thus alone?"

"I am in God's hands," replied Luther. "He is my strength and my shield. What can man do unto me?"

The stranger turned pale and fled trembling.

Serra Longa wrote to the Elector: "Let not Luther find an asylum in the States of your Highness; let him be rejected of all, and stoned in the face of Heaven; that will be more pleasing to me than if I received ten thousand crowns from you."

The storm was gathering over his head, but more especially in the direction of Rome was it expected to burst. But while the distant murmurs of the storm might be heard, God aroused the German nobles to form a bulwark for His servant. Sylvester Schaumburg, one of the most powerful knights of Franconia, sent his son with a letter for the reformer. "Your life is in danger," he wrote. "If the support of the electors, princes, or magistrates fails you, I entreat you to beware of going to Bohemia, where in former times learned men have had much to undergo; rather come to me. God willing, I shall soon have collected more than a hundred gentlemen, and with their help I shall be able to protect you, from every danger."

Letters of sympathy also reached him from many noble-minded men of that age.

When Luther received these letters, he exclaimed, "The Lord reigns, I see Him there, as if I could touch Him."

At this time the writings of the reformer were read

The Papal Bull

and his words treasured in cottages and convents, in the homes of the citizens and in the castles of the nobles, in the universities and in the palaces of kings. He now issued his famous "Appeal to His Imperial Majesty, and to the Nobility of the German Nation, on the Reformation of Christianity." In this he boldly condemned the false doctrines and bad practices of the Romish Church, and even went so far as to speak of the Pope as Antichrist. In a short time over 4,000 copies were sold.

The storm burst. The Pope issued a bull. Luther was given sixty days to forward his recantation. Failing to do this, he would be condemned, with all his adherents, as open and obstinate heretics.

Dr. Eck rejoiced, and brought the bull into Germany. Little encouragement was given to him as he advanced. The bull was treated as his bull, and was attributed to private revenge. In many places the German people tore it down and trampled it underfoot, and at Erfurt the students threw the copies they obtained into the river. Several of the bishops refused to publish it. But grave danger threatened the reformer. If the mighty hand of the Emperor united with that of the Pope, who could save the poor monk? For centuries the sentence of excommunication had been followed by death. What would Luther do? All eyes were turned toward him. While the bull was on its way he published his tract on "The Babylonian Captivity of the Church," closing it with these words: "I hear that new papal excommunications have been concocted against me. If it be so, this book may be considered as a part of my recantations. The rest will follow shortly in proof of my obedience, and the complete work will, by Christ's help, form such a whole as Rome has never yet seen or heard of."

On October 3 the bull was published. Upon hearing of this, Luther said, "I despise it, and attack it as impious, false, and in every respect worthy of Eck." A month later he issued his treatise "Against the Bull of Antichrist." But a still more daring step was held in reserve. On November 17, he again appealed, in the presence of a notary and five witnesses, from the Pope to a General Christian Council hereafter to be held.

On December 10, a placard was fixed to the walls of the University of Wittenberg, inviting the professors and students to be present at nine o'clock the following morning at the east gate. A large number assembled. Luther led the way to the appointed spot. A fire was lighted, and as the flames rose high into the air he approached and cast the canonical law books, some writings of Eck's, and the Pope's bull into the fire, saying as he did so, "Since thou hast vexed the Holy One of the Lord, may everlasting fire vex and consume thee."

By this bold act he broke down the bridge of retreat; henceforth he must go onward or die. Great efforts were now made by the papal party to obtain from the Emperor an edict sentencing Luther to death. But Charles V referred the papal nuncios to the Elector of Saxony.

The Papal Bull

The importance of winning over the Elector to their side was fully estimated by Luther's enemies, and an interview with that prince was sought. "In your Highness are reposed all our hopes for the salvation of the Church and the Holy Roman Empire," pleaded Aleander the nuncio. Then he added with great vehemence, "Unless a remedy be speedily applied the empire is ruined. I require two things of you in the name of his Holiness: first, that you will burn Luther's writings; secondly, that you will inflict on him the punishment he deserves, or at least that you will deliver him to the Pope."

The Elector took time to reply to this violent speech. He was placed in a difficult position. He feared to offend the Pope, and he shrank from delivering up one whom he had long befriended. A youthful voice pleaded for the reformer. John Frederick, the Elector's nephew, then seventeen years of age, wrote to his uncle on Luther's behalf.

The Elector was just, and refused to give way to the wishes of the Pope. He replied to the nuncios that not any other person had shown that Luther's writings had been refuted and deserved to be thrown into the fire. He requested Doctor Luther should be furnished with a safe-conduct, so that he might appear before a tribunal of learned, pious, and impartial judges.

But while the agents of Rome were trying their utmost to destroy the reformer, Germany was overwhelming him with acclamations. Although the plague was raging in Wittenberg, new students arrived every day, and from four to six hundred disciples habitually sat at the feet of Luther and Melancthon. The two churches that belonged to the convent and the town were not large enough to hold the crowds who came to hear the reformer. Princes, nobles, and learned men from every quarter wrote him letters full of consolation and faith. But some of his friends grew timid, and seemed about to leave him. Staupitz was one of these. To him Luther wrote, "You exhort me to be humble, I exhort you to be firm."

> God will keep His own anointed,
>   Naught shall harm them, none condemn,
> All their trials are appointed,
>   All must work for good to them;
> All shall help them
>   To their heavenly diadem.

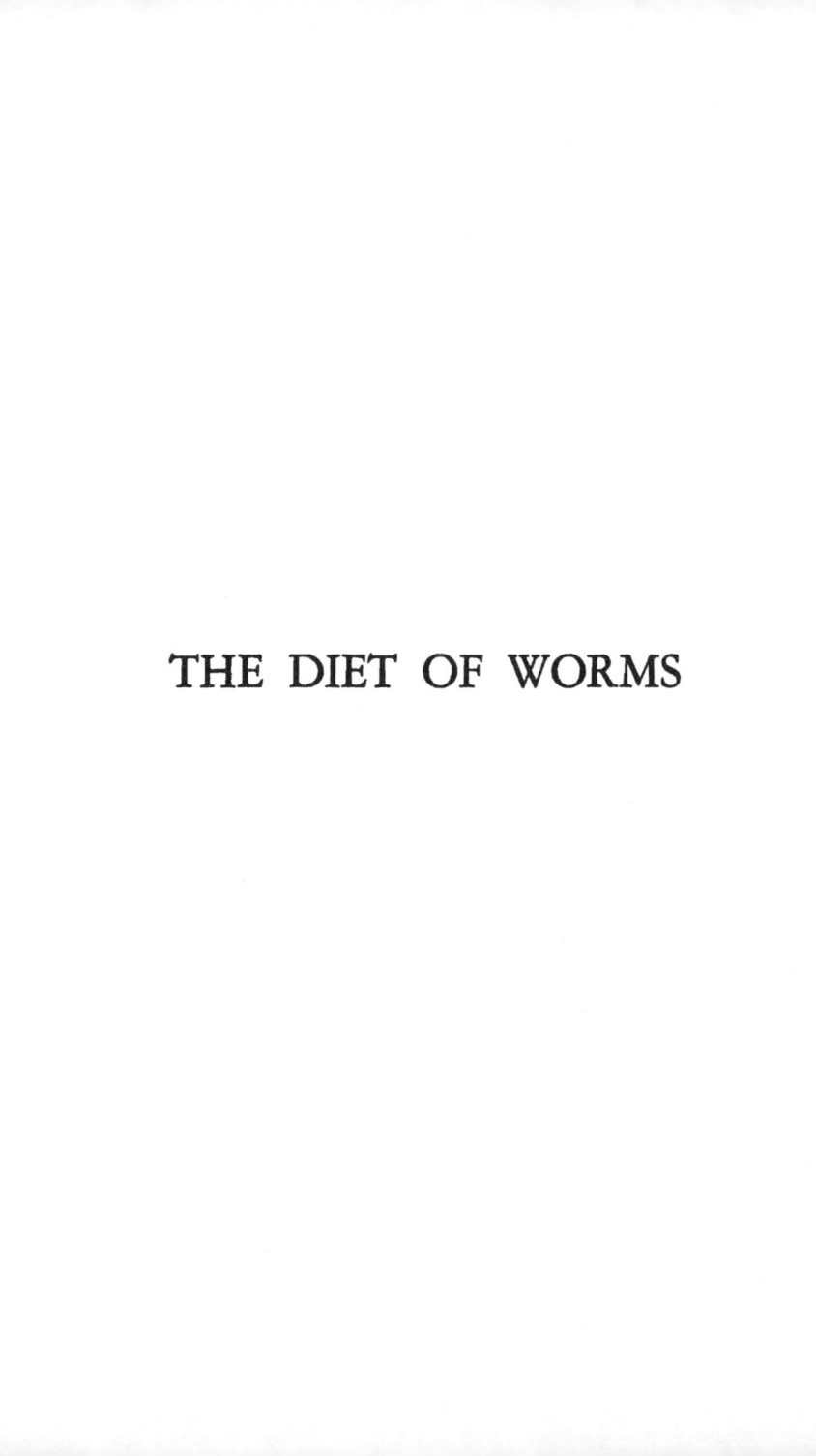

THE DIET OF WORMS

Chapter 11

THE DIET OF WORMS

And ye shall be brought before governors and kings for my sake, for a testimony against them.— Matt. 10:18.

WE NOW COME TO the grandest scene in Luther's life—his appearance before the Diet of Worms. Nuremberg, where the Diet should have been held, was suffering from the plague, so it was summoned to meet at Worms on January 6, 1521.

All the princes wished to be present, and as they journeyed along the roads leading to the city, the chief topic of conversation was the cause of the monk of Wittenberg. Important business connected with the empire was to be transacted; but the principal subject for discussion, it was understood, would be the Reformation.

In his desire to please both the Pope and the Elector, the Emperor requested Frederick to bring Luther with him to the Diet. This request perplexed the Elector, who feared that at any moment the alliance of the Pope might become necessary to Charles V and then the reformer would be sacrificed. Spalatin communicated the contents of the letter to Luther. His friends were alarmed, but he did not tremble. His health was very weak, but that did not matter. He looked upon the call as coming from God. "If I cannot go to Worms in good health," he wrote to the Elector, "I will be carried there weak as I am. If they desire to use violence against me, which is very probable, I place the matter in the Lord's hands. He still lives and reigns who preserved the three young men out of the burning fiery furnace. If He will not save me, my life is of very little consequence. You may expect anything from me except flight and recantation. Fly, I cannot, and still less retract."

Before this letter reached him Frederick had set out for Worms without the reformer.

The Diet was opened on January 28, 1521. The papal nuncios did not want Luther at Worms. What evils might not arise to the papacy from the presence of the monk, with his powerful eloquence! A second bull was therefore issued by the Pope; the former threatened Luther with excommunication, this pronounced the sentence against him and his adherents. Every nerve was strained, and intrigues resorted to by the papal party, to prevail upon the Emperor to issue a stringent edict enforcing this bull; and Charles V prepared one, which he laid before the assembled princes.

It was, however, necessary to gain over the Diet. Aleander undertook the task. For three hours he pleaded, with all the eloquence of which he was master; he even offered himself to be burned if only the monster Luther could be burned with him. "Fear

The Diet of Worms

not," he said; "in Luther's errors there is enough to burn a hundred thousand heretics. Let the axe be laid to the root of this poisonous tree."

The effect upon the assembly was great, but it quickly passed away. It was resolved that the reformer should appear before the Diet; and safe-conducts were eventually granted to him by the Emperor and by those princes through whose territories he would have to pass.

The summons to appear was handed to Luther by the imperial herald on March 24. Would he obey it?

The Elector wrote to his brother: "Doctor Martin has been summoned here, but I do not know whether he will come. I cannot augur any good from it."

But Luther had been called, and he would go!

On April 2 he took leave of his friends. Turning to Melancthon he said, "My dear brother, if I do not return, and should my enemies put me to death, continue to teach, and stand fast in the truth." Then, commending himself to God, he got into the car provided for him by the town council, and, amid the prayers and tears of friends and citizens, set out upon his perilous journey.

Preceded by the herald, carrying the imperial eagle, and accompanied by his friends Schurff, Amsdorff, and Suaven, he pressed onward. Gloomy fears filled the hearts of all whom he met. At Naumburg, a priest held before him a portrait of Savonarola, who had been burned a few years previously. At Weimar his ears were greeted with the cries of the people as they watched the messenger posting up an edict which the

Emperor had issued, commanding that his writings should be given up to the magistrates.

From Weimar, where he preached, he proceeded to Erfurt. As he was approaching that town he was received by a body of senators and distinguished friends, who escorted him within its walls. Passing onward, now accompanied by Justus Jonas, a most powerful preacher, as well as by his other friends, he reached Eisenach, where he was taken seriously ill. A night's rest, however, restored him, and he was able on the following day to continue his journey.

As he went along, crowds of people flocked around him. They gazed with emotion upon the intrepid monk. "Ah!" said some, "there are so many bishops and cardinals at Worms, they will burn you as they did John Huss." Nothing daunted, he replied, "Though they should kindle a fire all the way from Worms to Wittenberg, the flames of which reached to Heaven, I would walk through it, in the name of the Lord, and would appear before them."

On Sunday, April 14, he entered into Frankfort, from which place he wrote to Spalatin desiring that a lodging might be prepared for him.

A plot was now devised by the papal party to draw him aside to Ebernburg until the safe-conduct expired; but through his firm determination to keep straight onward, it was foiled.

Spalatin, who was with the Elector at Worms, trembling for the result of the reformer's appearance in that city, sent a special messenger entreating him to beware of proceeding farther. To this messenger he

The Diet of Worms

answered, "Go and tell your master, that even should there be as many devils in Worms as tiles upon the house tops, still I would enter it!"

At length, on the morning of April 16, Luther saw the walls of the ancient city. The people were anxiously expecting him. An escort, composed of young nobles, knights, and gentlemen, rode out to meet him. A great crowd was waiting at the gates of the city, and two thousand persons accompanied him through its streets.

The news of his arrival filled both the Emperor and the papal nuncios with alarm. Charles V immediately summoned his council. "Luther is come," said he, "what must we do?" Rome gave an answer. She gave advice which had already been tried. "Let your Imperial Majesty get rid of the man at once," said the Bishop of Palermo. "Did not Sigismund cause John Huss to be burned? We are not bound either to give or to observe the safe-conduct of a heretic." "No!" said Charles, "we must keep our promise."

The next morning, Luther was summoned to appear at four o'clock in the afternoon before his Imperial Majesty and the States of the Empire. The hour approached. For a moment this intrepid soldier of Christ felt dismayed, as he thought of the august assembly before which he had to appear; but he pleaded with God, and strength was given. At four o'clock he followed the imperial herald and the marshal of the empire to the Town Hall. Crowds thronged the streets, all the windows were occupied and the tops of the houses covered with spectators; the people completely blocked the way, and the herald, seeing the difficulty of advancing, led Luther through some private houses and gardens to the place where the Diet was sitting.

He stood before the door which was to admit him into the presence of his judges. As he was about to pass through, a kindly hand tapped him on the shoulder, and the valiant old knight—the hero of many battles—George Freundsberg, said, "Poor monk, poor monk! thou art now going to make a nobler stand than I or any other captains have ever made in the fiercest of our battles. But if thy cause is just, and thou art sure of it, go forward in God's name, and fear nothing. God will not forsake thee!"

The doors were passed, and Luther stood in the presence of the Diet. Never had man appeared before a more imposing assembly. Seated upon the throne was Charles V. Surrounding him were the Archduke Ferdinand, six electors, dukes, margraves, archbishops and bishops, princes, the papal nuncios, and ambassadors—in all above two hundred. Such was the court before which the reformer stood.

For a moment he was somewhat awed. One of the princes, seeing this, whispered kindly, "Fear not them which kill the body, but are not able to kill the soul."

He approached and stood before the throne of the Emperor. Silence prevailed for a moment. Then the chancellor to the Archbishop of Treves said, in a clear loud voice, "Martin Luther! his Sacred Majesty has cited you before his throne to require you to answer two questions: First, Do you acknowledge these books," pointing to about twenty volumes placed on a table, "to have been written by you? Second, Are you prepared to retract these books and their contents; or do you persist in what you have advanced in them?"

After the titles of the books had been read, Luther made answer to the first question by stating that the books named were his. As the second question concerned faith and the salvation of souls, he entreated that his Imperial Majesty would allow him time so that he might answer without offending against the Word of God.

As the reformer had spoken in a respectful manner and in a low tone of voice, many thought that he hesitated, and even that he was dismayed. Charles V, who had never taken his eyes off him, turned to one of his courtiers and said with disdain, "Certainly this man will never make a heretic of me."

Luther's request was granted on the condition that he make his reply on the following day, orally and not in writing.

The Imperial herald conducted him back to his hotel.

The early part of the following day was spent in earnest prayer and in reading the Scriptures. As the hour approached for him to appear again in the presence of the Diet, he drew near the Word of God, which lay open upon the table. With deep emotion, placing his left hand upon the sacred volume and raising his right toward Heaven, he swore to remain faithful to the gospel, and freely to confess his faith, even should he seal his testimony with his blood.

At four o'clock the herald appeared to conduct him to the Diet. After waiting for two hours, surrounded by a dense crowd, which rocked back and forth like the sea in a storm, he was admitted, and again stood before the throne of the Emperor, calm and confident.

The chancellor having asked for a reply, Luther answered in a speech which lasted two hours. Speaking in German, he stated that he was the author of the books attributed to him. Modestly, but with energy and firmness, he declared that as soon as it could be proved by the writings of the prophets and apostles that he had erred, he would retract every error and cast his books into the fire. But unless he was thus convinced of error, he could not retract. This speech he repeated in Latin.

When he had ceased speaking, the chancellor of Treves said indignantly, "You have not answered the question put to you. You are required to give a clear and precise answer; will you, or will you not retract?"

"Since your most Serene Majesty and your High Mightinesses require from me a clear, simple, and precise answer," replied Luther, "I will give you one, and it is this: I cannot submit my faith either to the Pope or to the Councils, because it is clear as the day that they have frequently erred and contradicted each other. Unless, therefore, I am convinced by the testimony of Scripture, or by the clearest reasoning—un-

The Diet of Worms

less I am persuaded by means of the passages I have quoted—and unless they thus render my conscience bound by the Word of God, I cannot, and I will not retract, for it is unsafe for a Christian to speak against his conscience." And looking round upon the assembly which held his life in its hands, he said: "Here I stand, I can do no other; may God help me! Amen!"

The assembly was motionless with amazement. The Emperor, recovering himself, exclaimed, "This monk speaks with an intrepid heart and unshaken courage."

As soon as the Diet had recovered from the impression produced, the chancellor said: "If you do not retract, the Emperor, and the States of the Empire, will consult what course to adopt against an incorrigible heretic."

Luther repeated: "May God be my helper; for I can retract nothing."

He then withdrew, but was soon called back again, and another effort was made to induce him to retract. But firm as a rock he stood, while all the waves of human power dashed ineffectually against him. "I have no other reply to make than that which I have already made," was his final answer.

It was now night, and Luther was conducted back to his hotel. As he went along the streets, escorted by two officers, some friends exclaimed, "Are they taking him to prison?" "No," said Luther, "they are conducting me to my hotel."

When he arrived at the hotel, the weary monk, surrounded by Spalatin and other friends, gave thanks to God. As they were conversing, a servant entered.

"My master," said he, "invites you to refresh yourself."

Luther was affected by this kindness. He said, "As this day Duke George has remembered me, so may our Lord Jesus Christ remember him in the hour of his last struggle."

The servant repeated the words to his master, and, when dying, Duke George remembered them.

Calling to a young page, he said, "Take the Bible and read to me." The page read those beautiful words of the Saviour, "Whosoever shall give you a cup of water to drink in my name, because ye belong to Christ, verily I say unto you, he shall not lose his reward." The dying prince was comforted.

The Elector was greatly delighted by the noble courage of the reformer, and he determined to protect him more openly in the future.

The next day, April 19, the Emperor ordered a message to be read to the Diet, which he had written in French with his own hand. In this he said: "A single monk, misled by his own folly, has risen against the faith of Christendom. To stay such impiety, I will sacrifice my kingdoms, my treasures, my friends, my body, my blood, my soul, and my life. I am about to dismiss the Augustine Luther, forbidding him to cause the least disorder among the people. I shall then proceed against him and his adherents as contumacious heretics, by excommunication, by interdict, and by every means calculated to destroy them."

Yet another attempt was made to get Luther to retract. This was undertaken in a kindly manner by

The Diet of Worms

the Archbishop of Treves, and by several princes who felt deeply interested in him; but he remained firm, and professed himself ready rather to lose his life than forsake the Word of God.

The Emperor was very indignant when he heard that this effort had proved useless, and exclaimed, "It is time to put an end to this business." He gave Luther twenty-one days, in which he was to return home, and forbade him to disturb the public peace on his road, either by preaching or writing.

Having taken leave of his friends, the reformer left Worms, on Friday, April 26. Twenty gentlemen on horseback surrounded the car, and a large crowd of people accompanied him beyond the walls of the city.

Luther's account of the proceedings at Worms is very brief. He wrote to his friend Lucas Cranach—"I thought his Majesty would have assembled some fifty doctors at Worms to convict the monk outright. But not at all. 'Are these your books?' 'Yes!' 'Will you retract them?' 'No!' 'Well, begone!' That is the whole history."

> Though numerous hosts of mighty foes,
> Though earth and hell my way oppose;
> He safely leads my soul along,
> His loving-kindness, oh, how strong!
>
> When troubles, like a gloomy cloud,
> Have gathered thick, and thunder'd loud;
> He near my soul has always stood,
> His loving-kindness, oh, how good!

THE WARTBURG

Chapter 12

THE WARTBURG

I will say of the Lord, He is my refuge and my fortress: my God; in Him will I trust.—Ps. 91:2.

WHILE LUTHER WAS PROCEEDING on his way to Wittenberg, the Emperor signed an edict in the Cathedral of Worms, in which, after stating that the reformer had rushed like a madman on "our holy Church," he went on to say: "We have dismissed from our presence this Luther, whom all pious and sensible men count a madman, or one possessed by the devil; and we enjoin that, on the expiration of his safe-conduct, immediate recourse be had to effectual measures to check his furious rage." The edict further stated that no one was to harbor him, to give him food or drink, or to furnish him by word or deed with any kind of succor whatever, under pain of incurring the penalties due to high treason. His adherents were to be imprisoned, and their property was to be confiscated.

Meanwhile, the subject of this terrible condemnation quietly journeyed onward. He preached at Eisenach, where, as a boy, he had been kindly received by the good Ursula Cotta. He visited his aged grandmother at Mora, and he traveled along a road skirting the woods of Thuringia. Seated in a wagon, with his brother James and friend Amsdorff, he passed through a hollow way near the deserted church of Glisbach. Suddenly a sound of horses' feet was heard, and five horsemen, armed and masked, rushed upon the little party. James Luther fled. The driver tried to resist; but one of the assailants, with a terrible voice bid him "Stop!" and threw him to the ground. A second seized Amsdorff, and kept him at a safe distance. The rest dragged Luther from the wagon. They threw a military cloak over his shoulders, and placed him upon a horse. All five assailants galloped off, carrying their captive along with them into the gloomy recesses of the forest.

The report spread rapidly that the brave monk had been carried off. Some rejoiced, but many were astonished and indignant. A cry of grief resounded through Germany: "Luther has fallen into the hands of his enemies."

To avoid being followed, the horsemen took first one direction and then another, until the poor monk was quite exhausted, and begged for a few minutes' rest. He was allowed to dismount, and drank some water from a brook which still bears his name. As soon as it grew dark his guards took a new road; and just before midnight they reached the foot of a mountain. On the top was an old castle called the Wartburg, surrounded by dark forests. The weary horses slowly ascended the steep path, and Luther was admitted within the gates. He dismounted in the court,

The Wartburg

and one of the horsemen led him into a chamber, where he found a knight's uniform and a sword. He was dressed in these garments, and enjoined to let his hair and beard grow. In the Wartburg he went by the name of Knight George.

The preacher of Wittenberg was now severed from his flock; the bold servant of the Most High, who feared not the face of man, was now a prisoner in a gloomy fortress. Was he in the hands of friends or foes?

Various reports were circulated. "Luther's body has been seen pierced through and through," reached the ears of his friends. "Alas!" they said, "we shall never see the noble-minded man again." At Wittenberg the grief was very great.

Suddenly startling news reached that town: "Luther is alive!" "Our beloved father lives!" exclaimed Melancthon, "take courage and be firm."

The news was indeed true. Luther was alive, but a captive. The Elector, seeing the fearful danger which surrounded the reformer, had planned his capture, so that he might be kept in safety from his foes.

The Reformation progressed, and, notwithstanding the edict of the Emperor, Luther's writings were read more and more.

While in the Wartburg, Luther was not idle. He wrote letters to his friends, dating them from the "Isle of Patmos," comparing his prison to the island to which the apostle John was banished. He secretly issued many tracts, and translated the New Testament into German. He also took great pains to improve his knowledge of both Greek and Hebrew, so that he might translate his intended version of the Scriptures more accurately. "Scripture without any comment," said he, "is the sun whence all teachers receive their light."

The solitary life now led by Luther did not suit him. He became weak and ill. His mind was depressed. Seated alone on the ramparts of the Wartburg, he remained whole days lost in deep meditation. He longed to be with his beloved people at Wittenberg, once again contending for the truth against its many foes. Strange imaginations became to him living realities, and the enemy of mankind—Satan—appeared to assume a visible form. On one occasion, while engaged in translating the New Testament, he fancied that he beheld the prince of darkness prowling round him like a lion about to spring upon its prey. Alarmed and vexed, he snatched up his inkstand and flung it at the head of his enemy.

Day by day the restraint imposed upon him became more and more unendurable.

Tidings also reached him from Wittenberg, which enabling him sometimes to rejoice, at other times causing him profound sorrow and anxiety. The Reformation was progressing, but the zeal of some of its supporters exceeded their discretion. While Luther rejoiced to hear that the mass had been declared to be unscriptural, and that, thirteen monks had been led to leave their cloister, he felt sad and indignant when he heard that, in his beloved town, the churches

The Wartburg

were being broken into, priests insulted, books carried off, and images taken away and burned.

Another source of disquiet was occasioned by false prophets who came from Zwickau. They declared that they had received direct revelations from God; they cast the Bible aside, and despised learning. Many were led away, the University became disorganized, and the work of the Reformation was imperiled. In this hour of danger there was a general cry for Luther; he was the only one who could bring order out of this chaos.

At the end of November he had paid a secret visit to Wittenberg, and now he resolved to brave all the dangers that beset him and to leave his retreat. The Elector was averse to his doing so, but he could no longer remain inactive amidst the scenes which were taking place.

On March 3, 1522, he bade farewell to the Wartburg, and set out for Wittenberg. When near Jena he was overtaken by a dreadful thunderstorm, and sought shelter at an inn called the Black Bear. Two young Swiss students were also traveling toward Wittenberg, and stopped at the same inn. Seated at a table, intently reading a book, was a knight who politely invited them to come and sit at his table, also offering them refreshment. Encouraged by his kindness, they said, "Sir, could you inform us where Martin Luther is at present?"

"I know for certain," answered the knight, "that he is not at Wittenberg, but he will be there shortly."

"If God spare our lives," said one of the young

men, "we will not return home without having seen and heard Dr. Luther, for it is on his account that we have undertaken this long journey."

After supper the stranger knight shook hands with the students, and said, "When you reach Wittenberg salute Dr. Schurff from me."

"Most willingly," they replied; "but whose name shall we give?"

"Tell him simply," said the knight, "that he that is to come salutes you."

The knight was Luther, who continued his journey until he came to the little town of Borne, near Leipsic, from which place he wrote to the Elector, informing him of his intention to return to Wittenberg. In this letter he entreated his prince not to protect him, as no sword could further the Word of God. "You must offer no resistance if men desire to seize or kill me," he wrote, "for no one should resist dominions except He who has established them."

> Press forward, and fear not; though trials be near,
> The Lord is our refuge,—whom, then, shall we fear?
> His staff is our comfort, our safeguard His rod;
> Then let us be steadfast, and trust in our God.

RETURN TO WITTENBERG

Chapter 13

RETURN TO WITTENBERG

The Lord is my light and my salvation; whom shall I fear; the Lord is the strength of my life; of whom shall I be afraid?—Ps. 27:1.

LUTHER ENTERED WITTENBERG again on Friday, March 7. Doctors, students and people, all alike rejoiced.

He preached the following Sunday, and crowds flocked to the parish church to hear their much-loved pastor again. Very gently he dealt with his flock—he called them "his own sheep"—telling them that "violence can never propagate the gospel; that must be done by the Word of God alone."

All were delighted. Schurff wrote to the Elector, "Oh, what joy has Dr. Martin's return diffused among us! His words through Divine mercy are every day bringing back our poor misguided people into the way of truth. It is clear that the Spirit of God is in him, and that by His special providence he returned to Wittenberg."

The tumult subsided, and quiet reigned. Liberty of conscience was established. Luther continued to reside in the convent, and to wear his monk's dress, but every one was free to do otherwise. The rule was laid down that nothing should be rejected unless it were in opposition to the Holy Scriptures.

Tranquillity having been restored, Luther sought Melancthon's assistance in finally revising his translation of the New Testament. The printing was carried on with great zeal. Three presses were employed, and 10,000 sheets printed daily.

On September 21, 1522, the first edition appeared. In a short time the whole of the 3,000 copies issued were sold. A second edition followed in December.

In vain the Pope and princes burned the Scriptures and forbade their circulation. The demand increased, and by the close of 1533 fifty-eight editions had been printed. Duke George said: "Even after I had prohibited the sale, many thousand copies were sold and read in my States."

The New Testament having been finished, Luther commenced and carried on a translation of the Old Testament. Henry VIII, the King of England, had Luther's writings burned, and wrote a book against the reformer, in which he called him a wolf and a viper. This so pleased the Pope that he conferred upon Henry the title of "Defender of the Faith," a title still borne by the kings and queens of England.

Leo X died while Luther was in the Wartburg, and the new Pope was named Adrian VI.

But burning books could not stay the progress of the truth. Monks continued to leave their cells, and became preachers, colporters, or engaged in daily toil. The colporters traveled throughout Germany, selling Bibles and tracts to the people; and preachers in the open air proclaimed the glad tidings of salvation.

Bitter persecutions now commenced. Duke George imprisoned the monks and priests who followed Luther. At Brussels, the first martyrs of the Reformation laid down their lives. Three young monks, named Henry Voes, John Esch, and Lambert Thorn, were led in chains to that city. When asked whether they would retract, they replied: "No; we will retract nothing; we will not disown God's Word; we will rather die for the faith." Esch and Voes were burned; and Lambert, who was terrified at the prospect of death, was taken back to prison; but soon he boldly confessed his faith, and died like his brethren.

Luther felt deeply for these noble young men, and composed the following verses in commemoration of their death:

> No, no! their ashes shall not die!
>   But, borne to every land,
> Where'er their sainted dust shall fall,
>   Up springs a holy band.
>
> Though Satan by his might may kill,
>   And stop their powerful voice,
> They triumph o'er him in their death,
>   And still in Christ rejoice.

In July, 1523, Adrian VI died, and Clement VII was elected Pope.

Many of the German princes now embraced the cause of the Reformation, among whom was Philip, the Landgrave of Hesse, who said: "Rather would I sacrifice my body, my life, my estates, and my subjects, than the Word of God." These princes favored the preaching of the gospel in their States, and boldly opposed the efforts of the papal party. The partisans of Rome became more and more enraged against the truth, and two rival camps began to be formed in the empire.

Dreadful scenes were now witnessed in Germany. The peasants, who for ages had been cruelly oppressed, had risen against the nobles. In vain Luther had written to them from the Wartburg, saying: "Rebellion never obtains for us the benefits we seek, and God condemns it. The devil is striving to excite to rebellion those who embrace the gospel, in order to cover it with reproach; but those who have rightly understood my doctrine do not revolt." Despite his warning, the peasants rose, and fearful cruelties were committed. No mercy was shown, and day by day things grew more alarming. At length two decisive battles were fought on one day, May 15, 1525, and the insurrection was subdued. Upward of fifty thousand perished.

Luther struggled hard against this rebellion. He prayed, he wrote, and, while the disturbances were still at their height, he traveled through the country calming men's minds and bringing them into subjection to the Word of God. None of the Elector's subjects rebelled.

The aged and pious Elector, the friend of Luther and the Reformation, died on May 5, 1524. Just be-

Return to Wittenberg

fore his death he destroyed a will in which he had commended his soul to the Virgin Mary, and dictated another, in which he cast himself entirely upon the merits of Jesus Christ.

Frederick was succeeded by his brother John, who was a firm friend of the Reformation.

On June 13, 1525, Luther married Catherine Bora (Katharina von Bora). The wedding took place in the house of his friend, Amsdorff.

Two years previously, a group of nine nuns lived in the convent of Nimptsch, near Grimma, in Saxony. While diligently reading the Scriptures, they realized their mistake in trying to serve God by shutting themselves away from the world. They wrote to their parents, saying, "The salvation of our souls will not permit us to remain any longer in a cloister," but their parents refused to receive them. Feeling in their own consciences that they ought not to remain, they left the nunnery in two wagons provided by friends. Knowing that they would find a friend in Luther, they stopped at the gate of his monastery at Wittenberg. "This is not my doing," he said, as he received them, and rejoiced at their escape.

Several persons offered to receive the nuns into their houses, and Catherine Bora, who was one of them, found a home with the family of the burgomaster of Wittenberg.

At that time Luther had no intention of marrying, and recommended Catherine as a wife to two of his friends. But his father urged him to marry, and, after much serious thought, he said, "I am determined to bear witness to the gospel, not by my words alone but by my actions. I'll content my father, and marry Catherine." At the time of his marriage he was living alone in the convent at Wittenberg, and had laid aside the dress and name of a monk.

John, the Elector of Saxony, made the convent a present to Luther and his wife for a dwelling-house.

He was very happy in his marriage. "His dear and amiable Kertha," as he called Catherine, made him a good wife. She loved him much; and when he was dejected, she would console him by repeating passages of Scripture; she also worked his portrait in embroidery.

About a year after their marriage they had a son, whom they called John, and the next year a daughter, who was named Magdalen. In all they had six children. The old convent became a joyous home, and often Luther and his Kertha would be seen sitting in the window, overlooking their beautiful garden, singing together sweet songs of praise. He was very fond of music.

But a dark cloud rested upon the bright and happy household. When fourteen years old, Magdalen became very ill, and died. Luther was overcome. Speaking of her, he said, "I love her well; but oh, my God, if it be Thy will to take her home, I must resign myself to Thee." When she was very near death, her father read to her from the twenty-sixth chapter of Isaiah and, falling upon his knees at her bedside, he wept bitterly, and entreated God to save her. She died in his arms, in the presence of her mother. He often exclaimed, "God's will be done! My daughter has still a Father in heaven."

Philip Melancthon comforted his friend in this hour of sorrow.

> I've lost the child I held so dear,
> Nor can I check the flowing tear:
> But when I view Thy mercy-seat,
> My meditation shall be sweet.
>
> 'Tis true I weep, but thou hast smiled;
> Safe in Thy arms faith sees my child;
> I flee to Thee, my loved retreat,
> And meditation shall be sweet.

CLOSING SCENES

Chapter 14

CLOSING SCENES

Be thou faithful unto death, and I will give thee a crown of life.—Rev. 2:10.

EIGHT YEARS HAVE PASSED AWAY since Luther stood before the Diet of Worms, and another Diet is about to meet in the city of Spires.

The Reformation has continued to spread, until not only the Elector and the young Landgrave of Hesse are faithful to its cause, but other princes, and thousands of the people, hold the truth dear to their hearts.

The papal party have made great efforts to get the Edict of Worms enforced against Luther and his associates; but through the fearless courage of the reforming princes their plans have been foiled, and it has been decided instead that until a General Council meets, the gospel alone shall be preached.

The Diet of Spires was opened on June 29, 1526. Ferdinand, King of Bohemia, and brother of the Emperor, presided. The friends of the gospel were outnumbered by the partisans of Rome, but their courage was unshaken. They opened the halls of their palaces for preaching the Word of God, and thousands congregated to hear the truth.

The Emperor had furnished Ferdinand with a decree, three months before, requiring that the "Church customs should be everywhere observed, and that the Edict of Worms should be confirmed." When this decree was laid before the assembled princes, many declared it was quite beyond their power to enforce it, and, although published, it was not carried out. The followers of Luther feared that persecution was about to begin again; but just as the Pope and the Emperor seemed on the point of uniting to crush the Reformation, they quarreled. The forces ready to march against Germany then turned aside to Rome, which city was sacked amidst fearful carnage in May, 1527.

The Edict of Worms was suspended, and a season of rest ensued. Each State was allowed to act in religious matters as it thought right, giving account to God and the Emperor alone.

During this peaceful interval Luther, Melancthon, Spalatin, and another named Thuring, went throughout the country visiting the churches, teaching, admonishing, establishing new schools, and instructing the teachers.

In 1529, Luther issued his Catechism, which, next to his translation of the Bible, was his most useful work. In 1530, he wrote to the Elector, "Our youth now grow up so well instructed in the Scriptures and catechism, it does my heart good to see and hear them. Young boys and little maidens learn to believe

Closing Scenes

and understand more of God and Christ than was formerly known in our cloisters and schools."

Peace having been concluded between the Pope and the Emperor, the Diet reassembled in March, 1529. A resolution was passed, by twenty votes against fourteen, by which the power granted three years ago to each State to regulate its own religious affairs was revoked, and all changes in the public religion were declared to be unlawful until the decision of the General Council should be known. This prevented the Reformation from being extended.

"Let us reject this decree," said the Lutheran princes. "In matters of conscience the majority have no power."

On April 18, Ferdinand appeared in the Diet, thanked the Romanists for their fidelity, said that the resolution, having been passed by a majority, would become an Imperial edict, and told the Elector and his friends that their part was submission. They retired to consult together, but Ferdinand would not wait. All entreaties were useless. "I have received an order from His Imperial Majesty," he said. "I have executed it. All is over."

But all was not over. The reforming princes drew up a formal protest, or declaration of their opinions, in which they appealed from the Diet to the Word of God, and from the Emperor Charles to Jesus Christ, the King of kings and Lord of lords. This protest they read before the Diet, and sent a copy to Ferdinand, who refused to accept it.

From that day the name Protestant has been given

to all those who hold the truth in opposition to the Church of Rome.

The Protest of Spires was followed in 1530 by the Confession of Augsburg, and, after a season of warlike preparation and great anxiety, peace was concluded between the Emperor and the Protestants in 1532, when Germany enjoyed a season of quietness for several years.

Now as to the closing scenes of the reformer's life. In 1529, the discussion was held at Marburg between Luther and Zwingli—the Swiss reformer—upon the presence of Christ's body in the Sacrament of the Lord's Supper. Soon afterward, feeling the need of rest, he requested permission to retire into the country. The Elector preferred that he remain at Wittenberg, and he resided in that town until a few weeks before his death.

In 1527 he was attacked by severe illness, and his life was despaired of. Thinking then that his end was near, he took leave of his wife and his little son; but he was not yet destined to die. From this time, however, he was frequently subject to a painful disease, which affected his head, and, toward the end, impaired his sight. Notwithstanding his increasing infirmities, he undertook a journey, in the winter of 1546, from Wittenberg to Eisleben, in the hope of settling a dispute which had arisen between the Dukes of Mansfeld and their subjects.

He set out on January 23 attended by his three sons. He reached Halle, but was so weak that his friend, Doctor Jonas, accompanied him for the rest of the journey. At Eisleben he was much worse, yet he preached four times, administered the Lord's Supper twice, and ordained two ministers. Until February 16 he attended all the meetings held for the purpose of arranging the debate and said, "If I can but succeed in restoring harmony amongst my dear princes and their subjects, I will cheerfully return home and lay me down in the grave."

On the 17th his illness increased. He spoke often of death and eternity, and prayed much. At night he complained of great oppression on his chest, and, feeling death approaching, he prayed, saying, "I beseech Thee, my Lord Jesus Christ, receive my soul. O Heavenly Father, though I be snatched out of this life, yet know I assuredly that I shall dwell with Thee for ever."

Then he exclaimed three times, "Father, into Thy hands I commit my spirit."

Doctor Jonas, said, "Venerable father, do you die firm in the faith you have taught?" He distinctly answered, "Yes."

Between two and three o'clock in the morning of February 18, 1546, he died. He had gone to be with the Saviour whom he loved so well.

His body was brought back to Wittenberg, and buried in the Church of All Saints. Dukes and nobles followed him to the grave.

Besides his widow, Catherine, he left behind him three sons and two daughters.

More than four hundred years have passed since Luther died, but he being dead yet speaketh. His firm adherence to the truth, his dauntless courage, his prayerful spirit and solemn regard for divine things, his faith in God, and his zeal in pursuing that which was right, speak to us from afar. His memory will ever be venerated by those whose delight is in the law of the Lord, and whose aim it is to do His will.

In 1821, William III, King of Prussia, ordered a monument to be erected to Luther in the market-square of Wittenberg, and in 1868 a magnificent memorial was inaugurated in the city of Worms. But Luther's best memorial exists in the noble work which he was called to accomplish, in the faithful translation of the Scriptures which he gave to Germany, in his beautiful hymns, and in the loving gratitude of tens of thousands of Christian hearts.

> Servant of God, well done!
>   Rest from thy loved employ;
> The battle o'er, the victory won,
>   Receive thy crown with joy.